THE WHOLE MAN

LUKE ST.CLAIR

THE WHOLE MAN

PRAYING OVER SPIRIT, SOUL & BODY

The Whole Man
Praying Over Spirit, Soul & Body

© 2024 by Luke St.Clair

Published by Truth Book Company, LLC
Anderson, IN

All rights reserved. No part of this publication may be reproduced, stored in a retrieval system or transmitted in any form by any means, electronic, mechanical, photocopy, recording, or otherwise, without the prior permission of the publisher, or author, except as provided by USA copyright law.

ISBN 979-8-9895526-3-4, paperback

Cover Design & Typesetting: Jordon P. Frye
Editing: Steven N. Gill & Jordon P. Frye

Scripture quotations from The Authorized (King James) Version unless otherwise noted. Rights in the Authorized Version in the United Kingdom are vested in the Crown. Reproduced by permission of the Crown's patentee, Cambridge University Press. Added emphasis has been noted.

We hope you enjoy this book from Truth Book Company. Our goal is to provide high-quality, Bible-based books, curriculum, and resources to equip you to stand for truth.

For more information on our other books and resources, special discounts, bulk purchases, or hosting a live event, please visit www.truthbook.co.

This book is dedicated to my beautiful wife, Tami-Jo, and our three amazing daughters, Lauren, Gracelyn, and Jocelyn. Thank you for your unwavering support in this effort.

Additionally, heartfelt appreciation goes to the 'Heroes of the Faith' who have consistently shown me the infinite value and deep significance of prayer throughout every stage of my life. Your steadfast walk with God has shaped my love and appreciation for communion with the Almighty. With a sincere heart, I humbly present "The Whole Man" as a tribute to each and every one of you. May its pages serve as an inspiration for others to embark on their own journey of daily prayer, and may it deepen their connection with the Lord, just as you have instructed me through your amazing examples in such an extraordinary way.

TABLE OF CONTENTS

INTRODUCTION

In the whirlwind of life's relentless pace, where daily demands often drown out the whispers of our souls, we find ourselves at a crossroads of spiritual neglect. Amidst this ceaseless pursuit, there emerges a potent yet overlooked tool—the practice of daily prayer. Welcome to "The Whole Man," a book that delves into prayer as an all-encompassing experience.

At its core, "The Whole Man" explores the transformative power of praying the Word of God—lifting His Word before His Throne. Scripture serves as our cornerstone for understanding prayer's holistic nature—a journey that addresses every facet from head to toe. Inspired by 1 Thessalonians 5:23, which recognizes man's three integral parts—spirit, soul, and body—we embark on a focused exploration.

"The Whole Man" is not just about discussing prayer; it urges us to actively participate in this transformative dialogue with the Divine, by lifting up and aligning ourselves with God's Word during our prayer time. It aims to eliminate any excuses that may hinder us from engaging in this sacred practice and invites us to enter sacred spaces for intimate conversations with the Almighty.

Throughout these pages, we will explore various methods and practical tools for incorporating scripture into our prayers and discovering what truly resonates with your heart. This book challenges misconceptions about time constraints and arcane skills associated with prayer while emphasizing how praying God's Word can bring transformation into every aspect of our lives.

Consistency matters more than length when it comes to prayer. Whether you spend five minutes or three hours praying before His Throne, maintaining a regular practice allows us to deepen our connection with Him and experience the power of His Word in our lives.

Release any thoughts of inadequacy or limited time and instead focus on cultivating a consistent rhythm—a discipline seamlessly integrated into the fabric of your life. This rhythm will gradually expand as you grow in intimacy with God.

In the stillness of daily prayer, "The Whole Man" unearths your dormant potential and invites you to bring your own practices into this sacred space. It encourages you to live out its manifesto—a dialogue that transcends uncertainties and hesitations—by actively lifting The Word of God before the Throne of God, engaging in heartfelt conversations with Him.

May this exploration guide you towards a deeper connection with God Almighty, embracing "The Whole Man" as an invitation to embark on an extraordinary journey where the power of praying the Word of God transforms every aspect of your life's story.

HOW I PRAY

In Luke 11:1, the disciples approached Jesus and asked Him to show them how to pray. This simple request holds profound significance, as it reveals their recognition of the importance of prayer in their lives. The significance and prominence of prayer is something that was deeply ingrained within me from my earliest days as a child.

Exploring the question "How do you pray?" matters because it shows that the person is genuinely interested in learning more about prayer. Just like the disciples who sought guidance from Jesus, I, too, had a longing to understand how to approach God through prayer.

My mother played a pivotal role in nurturing my spiritual journey. She lovingly created a prayer book for me, filled with scripture that served as a life-giving source. It became more than just a book; it became an instrument through which I could connect with God on a personal level.

I can still vividly recall those moments when I would take my little prayer book down to the basement of our old church building. As tears streamed down my face, I poured out my heart in prayer. The act of writing in that book and presenting my requests before God held immense power and meaning for me.

With each answered prayer, I witnessed miracles unfolding before my eyes. Gratitude overflowed from within me as I marked off those answered requests—a tangible testament to God's faithfulness and love and the power of prayer.

Prayer is not merely reciting words or going through motions. It is an intimate form of communication with our Heavenly Father. Through prayer, we express our deepest desires, fears, hopes, and gratitude directly to Him. It is through this sacred connection that we establish an unbreakable bond with God—one that transcends time and space.

So How Do I Pray?

As time went on, I continued to pray with a prayer book. However, as I grew older, my approach to prayer began to evolve. One particular model that resonated with me was the Tabernacle model. For many years now, I have personally prayed using this framework.

I am not alone in this practice; there are others who also find value in praying through the Tabernacle model. My mother embraced this method of prayer at times through the years, and so did Bishop G.A. Mangun (1919-2010). Bishop Anthony Mangun and even renowned South Korean Pastor David Yonggi Cho (1936-2021)[1] have both shared incredible insights on praying through the Tabernacle.

[1]Pastor David Cho was the pastor of the world's largest Christian congregation with a membership of 830,000 as of 2007. "O come all ye faithful." Special Report on Religion and Public Life. The Economist.

The Tabernacle model offers a structured approach to prayer that allows us to engage with God in specific ways. It draws inspiration from the biblical concept of the Tabernacle—a sacred dwelling place where God's presence resided among His people.

By following this model, we can navigate through various aspects of prayer, each representing a different stage in our spiritual journey. We begin in the outer court, at the gate, with praise and thanksgiving. Ultimately, we stand with Him in His presence at the mercy seat in the Holy of Holies.

In the **Outer Court** (Gate), we approach God with gratitude and adoration, recognizing His goodness and faithfulness. We express our thanksgiving for His blessings and lift up our voices in praise.

At the **Brazen Altar**, we confront our shortcomings and seek forgiveness for our sins. We humbly acknowledge our need for repentance, asking God to cleanse us from all unrighteousness.

Moving to the **Laver**, we engage in self-reflection and allow God's Word to wash over us. Here, we experience spiritual renewal, as we examine ourselves before Him.

The **Holy Place** within the Tabernacle model holds significant elements such as the Golden Candlestick, the Altar of Incense, and the Table of Shewbread. Each of these components carries symbolic meaning and provides deeper insights into our prayer life.

The **Golden Candlestick** (seven lights) represents illumination and spiritual enlightenment. It serves as the sole source of light in the darkness of the Holy Place. This reminds us of how important it is to seek God's guidance and wisdom as we navigate through life's challenges. Through prayer, we can ask for His divine light to shine upon our path (Psalm 119:105).

Isaiah 11:2-5 describes the sevenfold Spirit of God, which includes wisdom, understanding, counsel, might, knowledge, fear of the Lord, and righteousness (holiness). These attributes are crucial in our prayer life, as we strive to align ourselves with God's will and receive His divine insight.

In your own prayer time within this realm (the Holy Place), it is wonderful to spend time praying for wisdom and understanding like King Solomon did. In 1 Kings 4:29-30, it is evident that God granted Solomon an extraordinary measure of wisdom that surpassed all others. By seeking this same gift through prayer in the Holy Place, we acknowledge our dependence on God's guidance, and express our desire to walk in His ways.

By engaging in prayer within this sacred space—the Holy Place—we can commune with God intimately, while seeking His illumination and wisdom. As I pray here, I ask for His divine light to shine upon my path.

The **Altar of Incense** signifies our worship and intercession. Just as incense rises up to Heaven, our prayers ascend before God's throne.

The **Table of Shewbread** represents sustenance and provision of His Word. Our Daily Bread! As we approach God in prayer within this realm, we acknowledge His role as our provider—both physically and spiritually. The Logos and Rhema Word of God is provided here.

Finally, in the **Holy of Holies**—the innermost chamber—we stand in awe before God's presence with a clean heart and pure motives. Here is where we make our petitions known before Him intimately. It is crucial that when approaching God with requests or desires in prayer, we align ourselves with His will, rather than asking selfishly or amiss (James 4:3).

By following these stages within the Tabernacle model during prayer—moving from gratitude, to repentance, to renewal, to intimacy—we create a framework that helps us approach God more intentionally, while fostering a deeper connection with Him.

Praying through the Tabernacle has indeed enriched my own spiritual journey, providing guidance, structure, and a deeper connection with God. While I could write an entire book on praying the Tabernacle, there are numerous amazing resources already available on this topic. So, let's move forward and focus on one specific area that holds great significance in the middle portion of my prayer time.

After I have visited the Brazen Altar, where I crucify my flesh (Galatians 2:20), and have prayed at the Laver where I invite the Lord to expose sin within me (Psalm 139:23-24),

I personally pray through the Commandments of His Word (Exodus 20:1-17). It is a moment of humble surrender, as I lay down my desires and selfishness before God—seeking His will above all else becomes my heart's desire.

Reflecting on each commandment that comes to mind from God's Word—such as loving Him with all my heart, and loving others as myself (Deuteronomy 6:4-5, Matthew 22:37-39)—I evaluate how well I am living according to these principles. This reflection allows me to seek alignment with His will for every aspect of my life.

After visiting these two significant places—the Brazen Altar and the Laver—I begin to pray for the WHOLE MAN and plead the blood of Jesus! This encompasses every aspect of who I am spiritually, mentally, emotionally, and physically, in complete surrender before God.

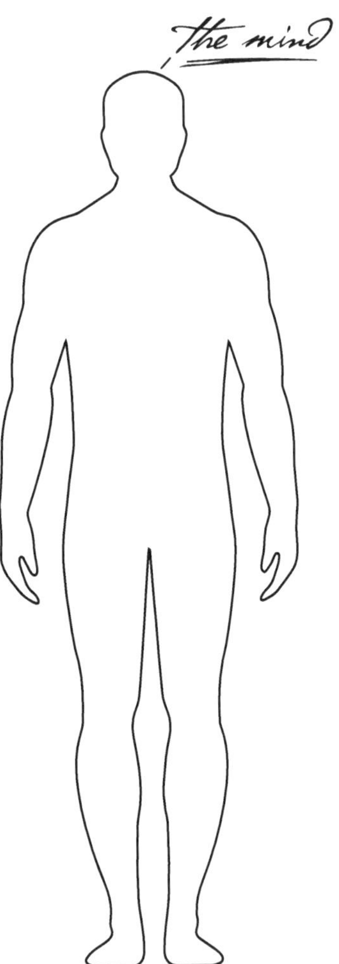
the mind

Prayer for

THE MIND

> *And the very God of peace sanctify you wholly; and [I pray God] your whole spirit and soul and body be preserved blameless unto the coming of our Lord Jesus Christ. — 1 Thessalonians 5:23*

According to 1 Thessalonians 5:23, we are comprised of three parts: spirit, soul, and body. Each part plays a significant role in our overall well-being—physically, spiritually, and emotionally.

Starting at the top of your head and moving down to your feet, while being covered by the blood of Jesus, is a powerful way to pray for every aspect of your being.

In a spiritual context, the mind is indeed a powerful tool—it shapes our thoughts, emotions, and actions. In many ways, it represents who we are as individuals.

Isaiah 26:3 says,

> *Thou wilt keep [him] in perfect peace, [whose] mind [is] stayed [on thee]: because he trusteth in thee.*

This verse reminds us that when our minds are anchored in God's Truth and filled with trust in Him, we can experience His perfect peace, even amidst life's challenges.

Renewing our minds through prayer and the study of Scripture allows us to align our thoughts with God's perspective (Romans 12:2). By intentionally focusing on and claiming His promises, and meditating on His Word (Psalm 119:15), we can overcome negative thinking patterns and cultivate a mindset that reflects His love, wisdom, and grace.

As I pray the Scripture personally over my own life and mind, I may say something like:

Lord, Your word says that You will keep me in perfect peace if my mind is stayed on You.

I surrender my thoughts and bring them under Your authority.

Help me fix my attention on You so that my mind may be filled with thoughts that align with Your Truth.

I ask for clarity of thinking and discernment as I navigate through life's challenges.

May my thoughts be guided by wisdom from above.

Please guard my mind against negative influences or distractions that seek to steal away my focus from You.

I trust in You completely and rely on Your strength to help me overcome any anxious or worrisome thoughts.

Thank You for granting me peace that surpasses all understanding as I keep my mind fixed on You.

I keep praying and personalizing the Word:

Philippians 4:8 - "Finally, brethren, whatsoever things are true, whatsoever things [are] honest, whatsoever things [are] just, whatsoever things [are] pure, whatsoever things [are] lovely, whatsoever things [are] of good report; if [there be] any virtue, and if [there be] any praise, think on these things."

THINK *on* THESE THINGS.

Philippians 4:8 provides a wonderful guideline for praying over our minds. It encourages us to focus on thoughts that are true, honest, just, pure, lovely, of good report, virtuous, and praiseworthy.

When praying this scripture for your mind, you can personalize it in the following way:

Lord, according to Philippians 4:8, You instruct us to think on things that are true, honest, just, pure, lovely, of good report; things that possess virtue and deserve praise.

Take some time to focus on each and every element:

- *True*
- *Honest*
- *Just*
- *Pure*
- *Lovely*
- *Good Report*
- *Virtue*
- *Praise*

I ask for Your help in aligning my thoughts with these qualities.

Lord, guide me in discerning what is true and honest, amidst the noise of the world.

Help me seek justice and purity in my thoughts by filtering out negativity and impurity.

Direct my attention towards things that are lovely, and of good report, so that I may dwell on positive aspects of life.

Grant me wisdom to recognize virtues worth pursuing and celebrating. May my mind be filled with thoughts worthy of praise—thoughts that bring honor to You.

I surrender any negative or unhelpful thought patterns at Your feet. Replace them with thoughts that reflect

Your Truth and goodness. Help me cultivate a mindset rooted in gratitude and positivity.

Thank You for being my source of guidance as I strive to think on these things. May they shape my perspective and transform my thinking according to Your will.

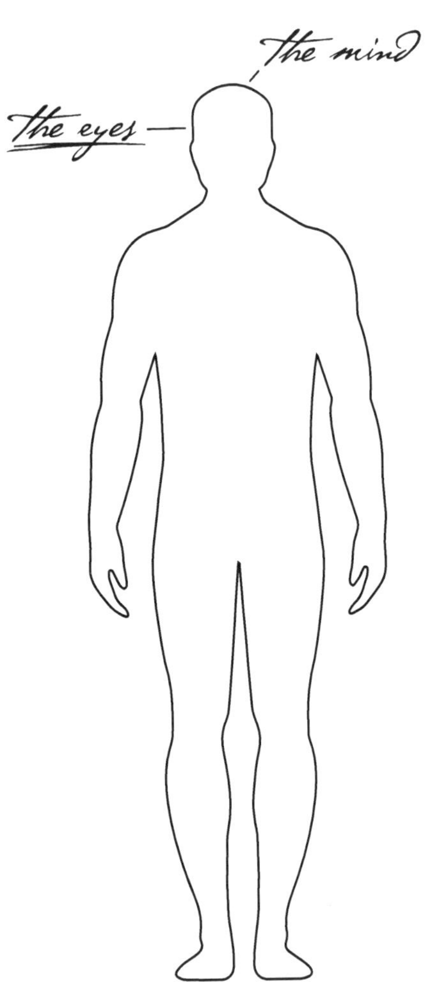
the mind
the eyes

Prayer for

THE EYES

It is truly amazing to witness the interconnectedness of every part of our physical body when we begin to pray using a diagram. After praying for my mind, I move down to my eyes.

In a spiritual sense, the eyes serve as a gateway to the mind and soul of a person. Unfortunately, they can often be a weak point in humanity.

In Psalm 121:1-2, David said,

> *I will lift up mine eyes unto the hills, from whence cometh my help. My help cometh from the LORD, which made heaven and earth.*

These verses remind us that our eyes need to be lifted towards God. We must set our affection on things above (Colossians 3:2). Often, it starts with what we choose to look at.

Psalm 101:3 states,

> *I will set no evil thing before my eyes.*

This verse encourages us to guard what we allow ourselves to see and behold. As a child of God, I must protect my heart and mind from being influenced by negativity or harmful content.

Let us remember that our spiritual well-being can be impacted by what we choose to fix our gaze upon. By seeking God's presence through prayer, and directing our vision towards His goodness and truth, we invite His light into every aspect of our lives.

As I pray over my physical body using this diagram and focus on my eyes, I recognize that they are part of the gateway to both my mind and soul, so I take some time here to pray prayers similar to these following prayers:

Precious Heavenly Father, I humbly come before You and ask for Your guidance in setting a guard at the gateway of my eyes.

Grant me discernment to filter and control what I allow myself to see.

Help me fix my gaze on things that are pure, uplifting, and pleasing to You. Strengthen me to turn away from anything that may lead me astray or hinder my spiritual growth.

May the things I behold reflect Your goodness and bring glory to Your name.

Just as David lifted his eyes unto You for help, (Psalm 121:1, Psalm 123:1) I too lift up my gaze towards You. You are where my help comes from. You are the maker of Heaven and Earth.

Lord, help me to "Set MY affection on things above, not on things on the earth" (Colossians 3:2). Help me to view the things that align with Your truth and goodness. Grant me discernment in choosing what I look at throughout each day. Empower me by Your Spirit, to resist temptation and avoid fixating on anything that is evil or harmful.

Lord, "I will set no wicked thing before mine eyes: I hate the work of them that turn aside; it shall not cleave to me" (Psalm 101:3).

Jesus, you said "That whosoever looketh on a woman to lust after her hath committed adultery with her already in his heart. And if thy right eye offend thee, pluck it out, and cast it from thee: for it is profitable for thee that one of thy members should perish, and not that thy whole body should be cast into hell" (Matthew 5:28-29).

Lord, Help me guard myself from the ***second look*** *of anything that would compromise my soul.*

the mind

the eyes

the nose

Prayer for

THE NOSE

In a spiritual context, the sense of smell significantly influences our overall well-being. It can impact the entire man. During the pandemic in 2020, one of the most prominent side effects of Covid was a loss of smell. If you have ever experienced losing your smell, you realize just how important our sense of smell truly is.

In the Old Testament, specifically in relation to the Levitical priesthood and their service in the Temple of God, it was crucial for priests to have an unimpaired nose (Leviticus 21:18). Sensitivity to smell was essential for a priest ministering in the presence of God. Like those priests, we too desire to stay sensitive to the Lord.

Just as certain scents can evoke memories and emotions, our spiritual "nose" plays a role in discerning God's presence and perceiving His leading. We want to be attuned to His fragrance—the sweet aroma of His love, grace, and truth—so that it permeates every aspect of our lives.

We need to pray that the fragrance of our lives is pleasing to God, rising up as a sweet-smelling savor before His Throne Room. May we cultivate sensitivity towards Him through prayer, worship, and meditating on His Word, so that we can fully experience His goodness and walk in step with His divine plans for us.

When praying personally over your nose and its significance, you can say something like:

Lord, as I continue praying using this diagram for my physical body, I recognize that my sense of smell greatly influences my overall well-being. It is dangerous to not be able to smell.

In Leviticus 21:18, You instructed that those who served in Your temple should not have a disfigured or impaired nose. This signifies how imperative sensitivity is when approaching You.

I desire to stay sensitive to Your leading and guidance in my life.

I also pray that the fragrance my life, and every aspect of my being will emit an aroma that rises into Your nostrils is a "sweetsmelling savor" (Ephesians 5:2).

Help me live a life that is filled with love, compassion, and righteousness, so that others may sense Your goodness through me.

the mind

the eyes

the ears

the nose

Prayer for

THE EARS

Among the various idiomatic expressions present in the New Testament, there is a particular figure of speech frequently used by Jesus. He consistently repeats the phrase "He who has ears to hear, let him hear" a total of fourteen times — six instances in the Gospels, and eight occurrences in Revelation. This expression holds significant meaning for Jesus and is closely connected to the wisdom traditions found within the Hebrew Scriptures.

In Proverbs 18:15 and 23:12, we observe a recurring theme — wisdom enters through one's ear and takes up residence within the heart.

During Prophet Ezekiel's divine calling into ministry, God instructs him to deliver his message regardless of whether his fellow exiles choose to listen or not (Ezekiel 2:5,7; 3:11). In this context, we find an ancient reflection of Jesus' saying as Ezekiel concludes with a similar thought from God:

> *Whoever will listen let them listen, and whoever will refuse let them refuse. — Ezekiel 3:27 (NIV)*

The Scripture emphasizes the importance of not only physically hearing, but also spiritually discerning and understanding God's voice. In a spiritual context, the ears of man hold great significance.

In a world filled with distractions and competing voices, it is crucial to cultivate attentive ears that are tuned to hear God's gentle whispers. Jesus said in John 10:27,

> *My sheep hear my voice, and I know them.*

This highlights the intimate connection between hearing His voice and having a personal relationship with Him.

By choosing to actively listen to God's guidance through prayer, meditating on His Word, and seeking His presence in stillness, we can discern His will for our lives. As we acclimate our spiritual ears to His voice, He leads us on paths of righteousness and reveals divine wisdom.

Let us guard our ears against being deafened by worldly noise or deceived by false teachings. Instead, may we prioritize listening attentively to the voice of God—knowing that as we do so faithfully, He knows us intimately, and guides us into abundant life. Pray things like:

Lord, Your Word reminds us of the power of hearing and listening.

Jesus, you said, "He that hath an ear, let him hear what the Spirit saith" (Revelation 2:7). As a matter of fact, Your word speaks of this principle over 58 times. Having physical ears does not guarantee that I am truly hearing what Your Spirit is saying.

I desire to position myself where I can clearly hear Your voice.

Help me be careful about what voices I choose to hear and entertain in my life.

Lord, help me guard against voices that would bring chaos and confusion into my life.

Your Word assures us that Your sheep know Your voice; You know them, and they follow You (John 10:27). I want to know Your voice, and I want You to know me. I will follow You Lord.

Lord, help me tune my spiritual ears to recognize and discern Your voice above all others.

Grant me wisdom to turn down the noise and chaos of life and a sensitivity to hear Your gentle whispers and give me courage to faithfully follow after You.

Lord, help me to quiet any distractions or worldly influences that may hinder my spiritual perception.

Thank You for giving me the gift of hearing, both physically and spiritually. May I use this gift wisely and be attentive to what You are speaking into my life.

the mind

the eyes

the ears

the nose

<u>the mouth</u>

Prayer for

THE MOUTH

> *Let the words of my mouth, and the meditation of my heart, be acceptable in thy sight, O LORD, my strength, and my redeemer. — Psalm 19:14*

Our words have the ability to shape our reality and impact others deeply. They can build up or tear down—bring healing or cause harm. Proverbs 18:21 reminds us that "death and life are in the power of the tongue." This verse is often misquoted as saying that the power of life and death are in the tongue. The scripture makes it clear that the power is not in life and death, but rather it resides within our tongues. Looking at this through a spiritual lens, the power of the mouth and tongue is immense.

Therefore, it is crucial to use our words wisely, recognizing their potential for both good and harm. By aligning our speech with God's principles—speaking truth with love, encouragement, and grace—we can foster positive change in ourselves and those around us. Our words become instruments of healing, reconciliation, inspiration, and transformation.

Let us be mindful of how we wield this powerful tool entrusted to us by God. May we choose words that uplift others' spirits, rather than tearing them down; offer comfort instead of causing pain; speak blessings instead of curses. In doing so, we manifest His love in our interactions with others—creating an atmosphere where hope flourishes and lives are positively impacted.

As you begin to pray over your mouth, try some of the following prayers and let The Spirit lead you as you pray:

Lord, I recognize the significance of praying specifically over my mouth and tongue.

My mouth has the power to get me into trouble quickly, and I acknowledge that I need Your guidance and help in this area.

Lord, death and life are in the power of my tongue; it matters what I say. (Proverbs 18:21)

Psalm 19:14 connects the words of my mouth with the meditation of my heart. May both my words and thoughts be pleasing to You, O Lord.

Help me guard against negative speech or harmful words that can bring destruction or hurt to others.

Lord, You said in Matthew 15:11, that what goes into the mouth is not what defiles the man, but that which cometh out. Don't let my words defile me.

Jesus, you taught us in Matthew 12:34, that "out of the abundance of the heart, the mouth speaketh." I understand that what comes out of my mouth is a reflection of what's in my heart. Therefore, I seek your transformation and purification within me, so that my speech may be edifying, encouraging, and uplifting.

Lord, please guide me in guarding my mouth.

Grant me wisdom to choose words carefully, to speak with kindness and love, and to refrain from gossip or hurtful language.

Help me use this powerful tool—the tongue—for good purposes: to speak life-giving words, offer encouragement, share truth with grace, and proclaim your love boldly.

Let my conversation always be full of grace and seasoned with salt, that I may know how I ought to answer every man. (Colossians 4:6)

Lord, give me utterance and help me to open my mouth boldly, to make known the mystery of the gospel. Let me speak boldly, as I ought to speak. (Ephesians 6:19-20)

Thank you for hearing this prayer and for helping me guard my mouth effectively.

the mind

the eyes

the ears

the nose

the mouth

the shoulders

Prayer for

THE SHOULDERS

> *Wherefore seeing we also are compassed about with so great a cloud of witnesses, let us lay aside every weight, and the sin which doth so easily beset [us], and let us run with patience the race that is set before us,*
> — *Hebrews 12:1*

From a spiritual perspective, the shoulders of a man bear the weight of both physical and metaphorical burdens. It is on these strong shoulders that we carry the weights that life places upon us. Just as Jesus carried His cross on His shoulders, symbolizing the ultimate burden He bore for our sins, we too face challenges and responsibilities that can feel overwhelming at times.

However, it is important to discern which weights are worth carrying. In Hebrews 12:1, we are encouraged to lay aside every weight and sin that hinders us in our race of faith. Sometimes, we may find ourselves shouldering burdens that were never meant for us—such as worry, fear, or unhealthy expectations.

By surrendering these unnecessary weights to God's loving care, and seeking His wisdom in discerning what truly matters, we can experience real liberty and freedom as we run this race that is set before us. Let us trust in God's strength to carry what is truly ours, while releasing the burdens that hinder our progress.

Pray things like this:

Lord, I come before You with a humble heart, seeking Your guidance and strength.

I pray that I would ***lay aside every weight*** *and the sin that so easily besets me.*

Help me to recognize and let go of anything that hinders my spiritual growth and slows me down in ***running*** *the race You have set before me. I am* ***looking*** *unto You Jesus, for You are the author and finisher of my faith. (Hebrews 12:1-2)*

Lord, I pray for strength in my shoulders to carry the loads that are too heavy for me alone.

Help me not to be weighed down by worry or anxiety, but to trust in Your provision and guidance.

Grant me wisdom to discern which burdens I should bear, and which ones I should surrender to You.

Teach me how to lean on You for support when my own strength falters. Your Word declares that Your grace is sufficient and Your strength is made perfect in weakness. (2 Corinthians 12:9)

May my shoulders be a reflection of Your grace and power at work within me. Help me remember that I do not have to carry everything alone, but I can cast my cares upon You, knowing that You care for me. (1 Peter 5:7)

Lord, I humbly ask that you would help me become a spiritual child of God that is ready and willing to bring restoration to those who have stumbled along the way and been overtaken in a fault. Help me to always approach them in the spirit of meekness. As I help others, help me to consider myself, lest I should also be tempted. "For if a man think himself to be something, when he is nothing, he deceiveth himself." (Galatians 6:3)

Teach me to ***bear the burdens of others****, "and so fulfil the law of Christ." Help me to prove my own work and find joy and fulfillment within myself, not seeking it from others.*

Give me the strength to ***bear my own burden.***

Father, do not let me be deceived; You will not be mocked: "for whatsoever a man soweth, that shall he also reap. For he that soweth to his flesh shall of the flesh reap corruption; but he that soweth to the Spirit shall of the Spirit reap life everlasting."

Lord, I pray that I would not be weary in well doing: for in due season I WILL REAP, if I faint not. (Galatians 6:1-9)

Thank you for being my source of strength when life's burdens become too much.

the mind

the eyes

the ears

the nose

the mouth

the shoulders

<u>the heart</u>

Prayer for

THE HEART

The heart of man, in a spiritual context, is a complex and powerful force. A heart full of deceit, pride, or wickedness harbors untold dangers. Issues of the heart, such as jealousy, anger, and unforgiveness, can lead to destructive actions. Guarding our hearts and seeking God's transformation is essential for a life aligned with His will.

When our hearts are surrendered to God, and filled with His love and Truth, they become wellsprings of life-giving goodness. A transformed heart overflows with compassion, kindness, forgiveness, and humility. It becomes a vessel through which God's grace flows into the world.

As we allow God to shape our hearts through His Word and Spirit, He replaces hardness with tenderness, and brokenness with healing. Our transformed hearts enable us to love unconditionally, as Christ loves us.

Let us continually seek after a pure heart—one that reflects Christ's character—and invite Him to examine our motives so that every beat aligns with His divine purpose.

Pray something along these lines:

Psalm 51:10-12 - *"Create in me a clean heart, O God; and renew a right spirit within me. Cast me not away from thy presence; and take not thy holy spirit from me. Restore unto me the joy of thy salvation; and uphold me [with thy] free spirit."*

Psalm 86:11 - *"Teach me thy way, O LORD; I will walk in thy truth: unite my heart to fear thy name."*

Father, I ask that as it is written in Psalm 119:34 that You would "Give me understanding, and I shall keep thy law; yea, I shall observe it with my whole heart."

Lord, "Let my heart be sound in thy statutes; that I be not ashamed." (Psalm 119:80)

I delight myself in You, Lord; and Your Word says that YOU will give me the desires of my heart. (Psalm 37:4)

Jesus you said, "Peace I leave with you, my peace I give unto you: not as the world giveth, give I unto you. Let not your heart be troubled, neither let it be afraid" (John 14:27). I am so thankful that my heart is full of Your peace and does not have to be troubled.

I pray that Christ may dwell richly in my heart through faith and that I am rooted and grounded firmly in love. (Ephesians 3:17)

Heavenly Father, help me trust fully in You with all my heart; and not lean to my own understanding, but in all my ways acknowledge You, and You shall direct my paths. (Proverbs 3:5-6)

With an upright heart will I praise Thee when I learn Your righteous judgments. (Psalm 119:7)

O Lord, do not despise a broken spirit and contrite heart within me—may this sacrifice be acceptable before You as declared by David's words from Psalm 51:17.

When you personalize these prayers like this example shows ("Lord, Your word says..."), it helps internalize them more deeply into your own spiritual practice.

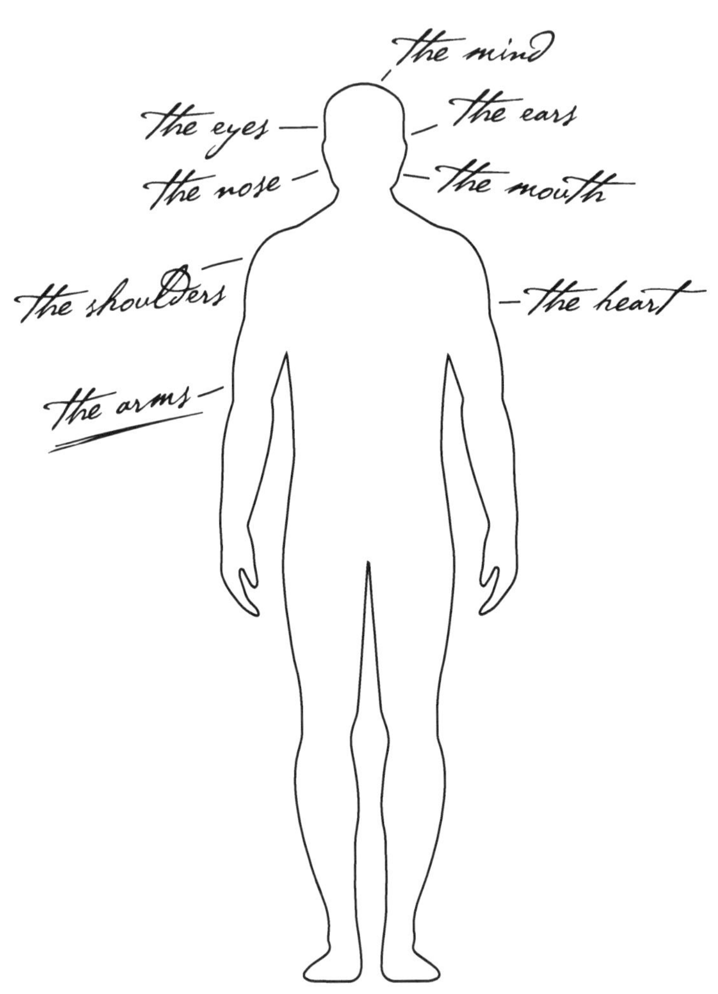
the mind
the eyes
the ears
the nose
the mouth
the shoulders
the heart
the arms

Prayer for

THE ARMS

In a spiritual sense, the function of arms represents our ability to reach out and embrace others with love, compassion, and support. They symbolize our capacity to serve, uplift, and offer comfort to those in need. Through our arms, we can extend God's grace in the world, spreading kindness and making a positive impact on others' lives.

The arms of the cherubim on the Ark of the Covenant were outstretched, covering the Mercy Seat. They represented God's presence and protection. This imagery symbolized His willingness to extend grace and forgiveness to His people, while also guarding and upholding His covenant with them.

Pray something along these lines:

Lord, may my arms continually be reaching towards heaven for strength, and reaching to my brother for unity, and reaching for the lost and dying that do not know you.

Father, strengthen my arms to carry out the work You have entrusted to me. Help me persevere and not grow weary in doing good. (Galatians 6:9)

Lord, Your Word declares that I have not chosen You, but You have chosen me, and ordained me that I may go and bring forth fruit, and that my fruit should remain. Father, may the work of my arms bear fruit that remains—a testimony of Your grace and provision (John 15:16). Use me as an instrument of Your love and blessing.

God, guide my arms towards acts of service that make a lasting impact on those around me. Your Word declares "As every man hath received the gift, even so minister the same one to another, as good stewards of the manifold grace of God" (1 Peter 4:10-11). Let every action reflect Your love and bring glory to You.

As Your Word declares, "…we have many members in one body, and all members have not the same office: So we, being many, are one body in Christ, and every one members one of another" (Romans 12:4-5). Lord Jesus Christ, unite our efforts as we use our individual gifts together—working harmoniously like different parts of one body—for the advancement of Your kingdom.

God, thank You for the ability to work with my arms. May I approach each task with a grateful heart, recognizing it as an opportunity to honor You. My prayer is that whatsoever I do in word or deed, I would do in all in the name of the Lord Jesus, giving thanks to God and the Father by him. (Colossians 3:17)

May these prayers inspire you as you seek to use your arms as instruments of service, love, and impact in the world around you.

the mind

the eyes

the ears

the nose

the mouth

the shoulders

the heart

the arms

the hands

Prayer for

THE HANDS

In a spiritual context, the hands of man hold great significance. They represent our ability to take action and make an impact in the world. Our hands can be instruments of love, compassion, and service, as we reach out to others in need. They can offer comfort, healing touch, and extend gestures of kindness. Just as God's hands are seen throughout Scripture as powerful and creative forces, our hands have the potential to bring about positive change and reflect His image.

When we align our actions with God's will, everything our hands touch becomes blessed. Whether it is through acts of generosity, or simply lending a helping hand, we have the opportunity to bring blessings into the lives of others. By using our hands for good purposes—lifting others up, working diligently with integrity—we participate in God's work on earth, and contribute to building a better world filled with love and justice. Here are some prayers to pray over your hands:

Lord, as I pray today, I want to lift up ***holy hands****, without wrath and doubting. (1 Timothy 2:8)*

Father, I pray that whatsoever my hand finds to do, that I would do it with all of my might. For there is no work, nor device, nor knowledge nor wisdom, in the grave. I want my hands to serve to the best of my ability. (Ecclesiastes 9:10)

Almighty God, let Your hand be upon me as was on men and women of old in Your Holy Word. Even as Jabez prayed "...Oh that thou wouldest bless me indeed, and enlarge my coast, and ***that thine hand might be with me****, and that thou wouldest keep me from evil, that it may not grieve me!" (1 Chronicles 4:10)*

Jesus, you said "Blessed are the peacemakers: for they shall be called the children of God." I ask that You guide my hands to be instruments of peace. Help me to pursue reconciliation, to extend forgiveness, and to promote unity in all I do. (Matthew 5:9)

Lord, Your Word admonished me to Fear not; for you are with me: to be not dismayed; for You are MY GOD:

You said you would strengthen and help me. You will uphold me with the ***right hand*** *of your righteousness.*

When I get weak, help me to strengthen my own hands. (Hebrews 12:12)

According to Your Word in Exodus 17:11, as Your People were fighting against Amalek, when Moses ***held up his hand,*** *Israel prevailed: and when he* ***let down his hand,*** *Amalek prevailed. Lord, Moses' hands became heavy and weary, and he needed the strength of Aaron and Hur to steady his hands. "...the one on the one side, and the other on the other side; and* ***his hands were steady*** *until the going down of the sun." (Exodus 17:12). Father, just as they lifted the hands of their leader, help me to lift the hands of my pastor so that he doesn't grow weary.*

Lord, Your Holy Word declares that, "The liberal soul shall be made fat: and he that watereth shall be watered also himself" (Proverbs 11:25). I pray that ***my hand will always be open*** *to share what you have blessed me with. I want to be a giver. I sincerely believe that as long as my hand is open, there will always be enough in my hands.*

Dear Lord, hear the voice of my supplications (earnest prayer), when I cry unto thee, when I lift up my ***hands*** *toward thy holy oracle (sanctuary). Draw me not away with the wicked, and with the workers of iniquity, which speak peace to their neighbours, but mischief (evil) is in their hearts. Give them according to their deeds, and according to the wickedness of their endeavours: give them after the work of their* ***hands****; render to them their desert. Because they regard not Your works LORD, nor the operation of Your* ***hands****, You shall destroy them, and not build them up. (Psalm 28:2-5)*

"O God, thou art my God; early will I seek thee: my soul thirsteth for thee, my flesh longeth for thee in a dry and thirsty land, where no water is; To see thy power and thy glory, so as I have seen thee in the sanctuary. Because thy lovingkindness is better than life, my lips shall praise thee. Thus will I bless thee while I live: I will lift up my hands in thy name. My soul shall be satisfied as with marrow and fatness; and my mouth shall praise thee with joyful lips:" Psalm 63:1-5

Lord, I will delight myself in thy commandments, which I have loved. ***My hands also will I lift up unto thy commandments,*** *which I have loved; and I will meditate in thy statutes. (Psalm 119:47-48)*

Lord, I pray that You bless the work of my hands, that everything I touch may prosper and be fruitful, according to Your will. "And let the beauty of the LORD our God be upon us: and establish thou the work of our hands upon us; yea, the work of our hands establish thou it." (Psalm 90:17)

the mind

the eyes

the ears

the nose

the mouth

the shoulders

the heart

the arms

the belly

the hands

Prayer for

THE BELLY

The belly of man holds symbolic spiritual significance. It represents the seat of desires, appetites, and emotions. Proverbs 20:27 reminds us that,

> *The spirit of man is the lamp of the Lord, searching all his innermost parts. (ESV)*

Our belly reflects our innermost being—our thoughts, intentions, and motivations.

It is crucial to guard our bellies against sinful cravings and selfish desires that can lead us astray. Instead, we should seek to align our desires with God's will and allow His Spirit to guide our hearts. By nourishing ourselves with Spiritual Truth, and cultivating a heart filled with love for God and others, we can experience true fulfillment in life.

Furthermore, Jesus spoke about rivers of living water flowing from within believers' bellies (John 7:38). This signifies the transformative power of His Spirit dwelling within us—bringing forth life-giving blessings not only for ourselves, but also for those around us.

May we continually surrender our bellies to God's transformative work, so that they become vessels through which His love flows abundantly into the world.

I love praying things like this:

Lord, You said in Your Word that "He that believeth on you as the scripture has said, That out of his BELLY shall flow rivers of living water" (John 7:38). Fill my innermost being with Your Spirit and let it overflow to bring life and blessing to those around me.

Just as David said it, "Bless the LORD, O my soul: and all that is WITHIN me, bless his holy name" (Psalm 103:1). Lord, let everything within me bless Your holy and righteous name today.

Heavenly Father, just as our physical bodies need food to sustain us, I pray that You would nourish my innermost being with Your Truth and presence. Jesus, You said that "Man shall not live by bread alone, but by every word that proceedeth out of the mouth of God" (Matthew 4:4). Let Your Word be like food to my soul.

Matthew 5:6 says, "Blessed are they which do hunger and thirst after righteousness: for they shall be filled." God, ignite a hunger and thirst for righteousness in my innermost being. Help me long for a deeper relationship with You and seek after spiritual growth.

Father God, strengthen me from the inside out, so that I can withstand trials and challenges. I pray today "That YOU would grant ME, according to the riches of YOUR glory, to be strengthened with might by YOUR Spirit in the inner man..." (Ephesians 3:16). Help me rely on You completely and find strength in Your presence.

Lord, Psalm 30:2-3 declares, "O LORD my God, I cried unto thee, and thou hast healed me. O LORD, thou hast brought up my soul from the grave: thou hast kept me alive, that I should not go down to the pit." Heavenly Father, bring healing to the deepest parts of my being—my belly—where emotional wounds may reside. Lord, I cry out to You for help and ask that You restore me from within.

Lord, I surrender my inner man to You—my thoughts, desires, fears, and dreams. Take control of all that is within me and guide me according to Your perfect plan.

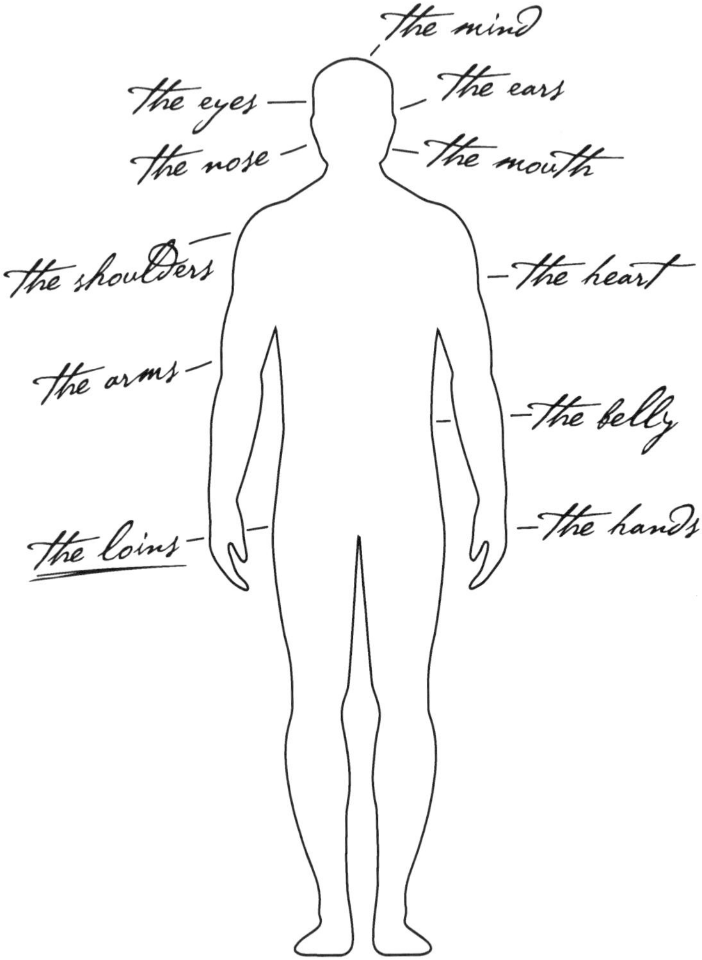

the mind
the eyes
the ears
the nose
the mouth
the shoulders
the heart
the arms
the belly
the loins
the hands

Prayer for

THE LOINS

From a spiritual perspective, the loins of man hold symbolic significance. They represent strength, vitality, and readiness for action. In Ephesians 6:14, we are encouraged to "gird our loins with truth" as part of the spiritual armor. This signifies the importance of being firmly grounded in God's Truth, and ready to stand against spiritual opposition.

The loins also symbolize procreation and birthing new life. In a spiritual sense, our loins represent what we are giving birth to, in the realm of faith—our dreams, visions, and God-given purposes. Just as physical offspring carry forward a family legacy, our spiritual endeavors can leave a lasting impact on future generations.

By nurturing seeds of faith within us, and allowing God's Spirit to work through us, we can give birth to acts of love, kindness, compassion, and righteousness that bring glory to God. Let us be intentional about cultivating fertile ground within our spirits, so that what is born from our lives reflects His goodness and transforms the world around us.

I also take time here to pray for my physical children/offspring.

Try some of these prayers:

Heavenly Father, I pray that You would strengthen me to gird my loins with Truth. Lord God Almighty, protect my loins from spiritual attacks by clothing them with your armor—truthfulness against deception and lies. (Ephesians 6:14)

Lord Jesus Christ, strengthen my loins physically so that I may have the energy and vitality to fulfill my responsibilities (Job 40:16). Grant me physical endurance as I serve You.

Lord Jesus, I don't want to be like the fig tree in Matthew 21:19 that had nothing but leaves — I want to bear fruit in my life. God of growth and transformation, nurture spiritual reproduction within me by helping me be like a tree planted by the rivers of living water that bears fruit in every season (Psalm 1:3).

Lord, heal any emotional wounds or burdens that may reside in my loins. Don't let my loins be filled with loathsome disease, where there is no soundness in my flesh (Psalm 38:7). Bring restoration and wholeness to every area of my life, so that I may experience Your peace and joy.

"I will open my mouth in a parable: I will utter dark sayings of old: Which we have heard and known, and our fathers have told us. We will not hide them from their children, shewing to the generation to come the praises of the LORD, and his strength, and his wonderful works that he hath done." (Psalm 78:2-4)

God, help me leave a spiritual legacy by imparting Your truth and love to future generations. May my children, and my children's children, walk in Your ways all the days of their lives.

If you have children:

Psalm 127:3-5 - "Lo, children are an heritage of the LORD: and the fruit of the womb is his reward. As arrows [are] in the hand of a mighty man; so are children of the youth. Happy is the man that hath his quiver full of them: they shall not be ashamed, but they shall speak with the enemies in the gate."

Gracious God, I thank You for the gift of children. I lift up my children before You, asking for Your guidance and protection over their lives. May they grow in wisdom, knowledge, and love for You. Bless my family with health, strength, and unity as we journey together in this life.

Lift the names of your children before The Throne one by one.

Heavenly Father, grant me wisdom and discernment as I guide and nurture my children in the ways of righteousness. Lord, help me to "train up a child in the way he should go: and when he is old, he will not depart from it" (Proverbs 22:6). Help me to be a godly example to them.

If you want children:

Heavenly Father, if it is Your will, bless us with fertility so that we may experience the joy of bringing new life into this world—help us to be fruitful, and multiply, and replenish the earth (Genesis 1:28). Guide us on this journey according to Your plan.

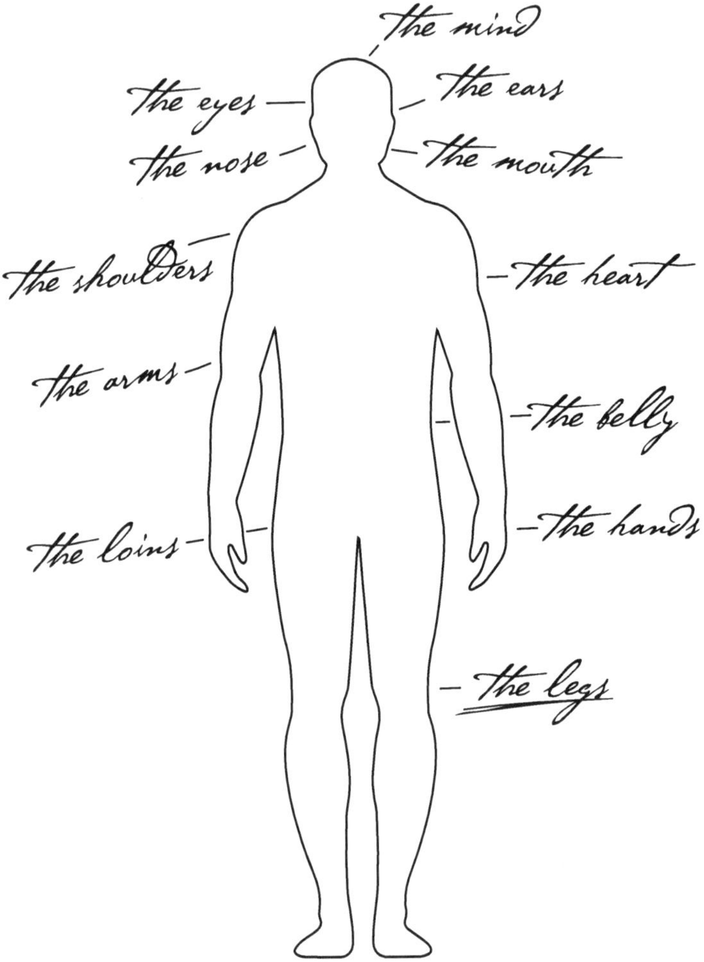

the mind

the eyes

the ears

the nose

the mouth

the shoulders

the heart

the arms

the belly

the loins

the hands

the legs

Prayer for

THE LEGS

In spiritual terms, the legs of a man hold profound symbolic value. They represent strength, stability, and what we stand for in our faith journey. Just as physical legs provide a firm foundation for our bodies, our spiritual legs ground us in God's Truth, and enable us to stand strong against adversity.

Our legs carry us forward on the path of righteousness, supporting our convictions and values. They empower us to take bold steps in living out our faith with courage and perseverance. By standing firm in God's promises, and aligning ourselves with His will, we become beacons of light amidst darkness.

Let us strengthen our spiritual legs through prayer, studying His Word, and cultivating a deep relationship with Him. As we walk steadfastly on this journey of faith, may our actions reflect the strength of character that comes from standing firmly on the solid Rock of Christ. Try some of these prayers:

Heavenly Father, I pray for strength in my legs to stand firm in my faith and walk according to Your truth. It is YOU that "girdeth me with strength, and maketh my way perfect" (Psalm 18:32). Strengthen me physically and spiritually to endure any challenges that come my way.

Lord, grant me courage like that of Caleb who wholly followed You (Joshua 14:8). Help me to be bold in standing up for what is right and true, even when faced with opposition.

Lord Jesus Christ, strengthen my legs to run the race set before me with patience and endurance (Hebrews 12:1). Help me persevere through challenges and remain steadfast in following You.

Lord God Almighty, help us stand firm against temptation and deception. "Lead me in thy truth, and teach me" (Psalm 25:5). Help me to walk in truth and share it with others.

Lord, grant me boldness like the apostles who fearlessly stood up for their faith despite opposition or threats, choosing obedience to God over human authority. They boldly proclaimed Jesus as Lord and continued sharing His message of salvation without hesitation or compromise. They STOOD "...with all boldness that they may speak thy word" (Acts 4:29).

Fill me with Your Holy Spirit so that I may boldly share the Gospel and stand up for righteousness and the convictions You have placed in my heart.

Lord, help me to STAND firm like Shadrach, Meshach, and Abednego regardless of who else is bowing down (Daniel 3:16). I will not bow down to the gods of this World.

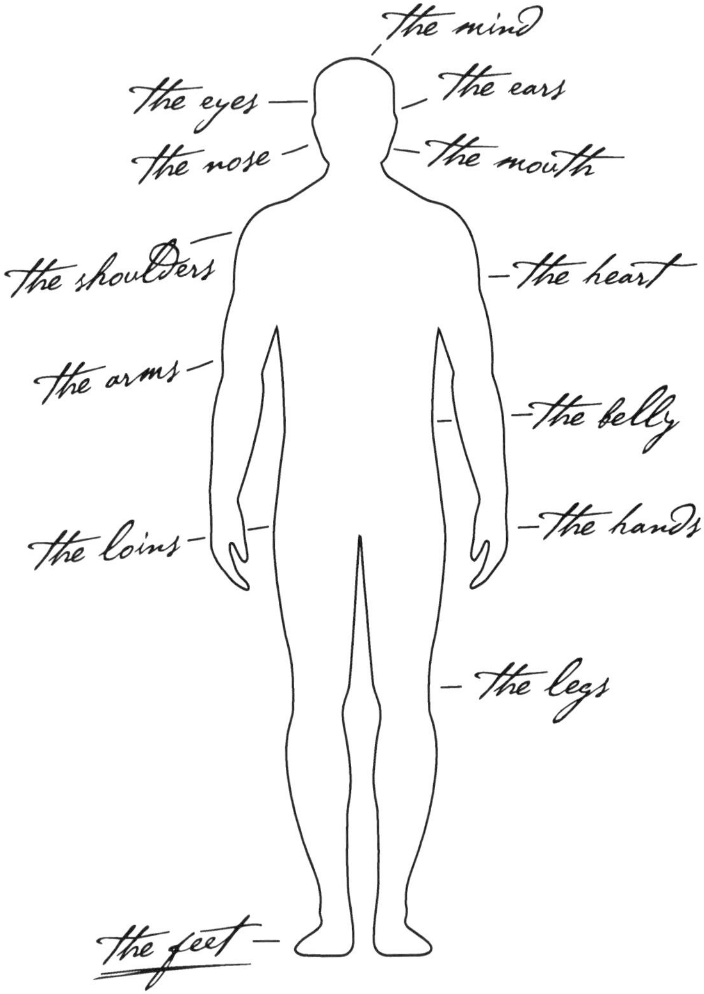

the mind

the eyes

the ears

the nose

the mouth

the shoulders

the heart

the arms

the belly

the loins

the hands

the legs

the feet

Prayer for

THE FEET

The feet of man are symbolically significant in a spiritual context. They represent our walk, our journey in life, and the paths we choose to follow. Just as God promised Abraham that every place he set his foot would be given to him (Genesis 13:17), our feet have the potential to take spiritual territory wherever they tread.

As believers, we are called to be intentional about where we step in the spiritual realm. By walking in faith and obedience, we can claim ground for God's Kingdom and bring His light into every sphere of influence. Our footsteps become a testimony of His grace and love.

Let us be mindful of the impact our feet can have on others, as we walk with integrity, humility, and compassion. May every place our feet touch become an opportunity for transformation—spreading God's Truth, extending His love, and advancing His purposes in this world. Here are a few powerful prayers to pray over your feet:

Father, let what was promised to Your children in Deuteronomy 11:24 be true for me as well. "Every place where the soles of my feet shall tread shall be mine." Grant me the ability to walk in dominion and authority, being filled with Your Spirit and called by Your Name.

Lord Your Word says, "The steps of a good man are ordered by the LORD: and he delighteth in his way. Though he fall, he shall not be utterly cast down: for the LORD upholdeth him with his hand" (Psalm 37:23-24).

Father, guide my steps towards the work that aligns with Your will and purpose for my life. Help me discern where You want me to invest my time and energy.

Lord, help me to "ponder the path of MY feet, and let all MY ways be established. Help me to turn not to the right hand nor to the left: and to remove MY foot from evil" (Proverbs 4:26-27). God, give me direction, guide my path as I walk on this journey of life. Lead me in the paths of righteousness for Your name's sake (Psalm 23:3), and help me make choices that align with Your will.

Lord, the Psalmist said, "But as for me, my feet were almost gone; my steps had well nigh slipped. For I was envious at the foolish, when I saw the prosperity of the wicked" (Psalm 73:2-3). Heavenly Father, I humbly ask that You guard my steps, preventing me from slipping and losing my way. Strengthen my faith, protect me from doubt and temptation, and guide each decision I make. Surround me with Your presence and provide a firm foundation for every step I take. Thank You for being a faithful God who watches over us.

Heavenly Father, let my actions bring beauty as I carry Your message of love and salvation to others. Your Word tells us in Romans 10:15, "...How beautiful are the feet of them that preach the gospel of peace and bring glad tidings of good things!" Use me as an instrument to share the gospel joyfully wherever I go.

Lord, I am praying "...that YOU would open unto us a door of utterance, to speak the mystery of Christ..." (Colossians 4:3). Open doors for me to share Your Truth and let my steps be directed towards those who need to hear it. Grant me divine appointments to bring hope and encouragement.

Lord God, "Hold up my goings in thy paths, that my footsteps slip not" (Psalm 17:5). Keep me steadfast on the path of righteousness. Help me walk faithfully in obedience to You, even when faced with challenges or temptations.

Heavenly Father, You have shown me "...what is good; and what doth the LORD require of ME, but to do justly, and to love mercy, and to walk humbly with thy God?" (Micah 6:8). Help me Lord, to walk humbly before You as I seek to follow Your ways. Keep my steps aligned with Your will, that I may bring glory to Your name in all that I do.

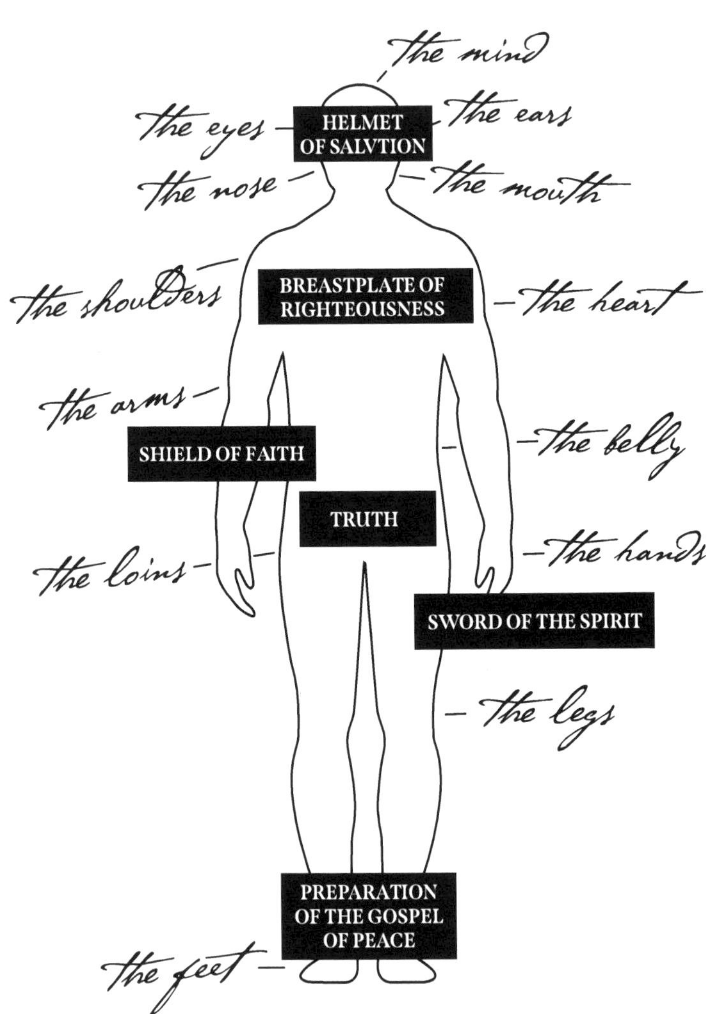
the mind
the eyes
HELMET OF SALVTION
the ears
the nose
the mouth
the shoulders
BREASTPLATE OF RIGHTEOUSNESS
the heart
the arms
SHIELD OF FAITH
the belly
TRUTH
the loins
the hands
SWORD OF THE SPIRIT
the legs
PREPARATION OF THE GOSPEL OF PEACE
the feet

The Whole Armour For

THE WHOLE MAN

Before concluding this season of prayer, I pray through Ephesians 6 once more, to ensure that before engaging in warfare, the Whole Armour of God is covering The Whole Man.

I have personalized the following verses for the sake of praying The Word:

Ephesians 6:10-20

In obedience to the words of the Apostle Paul…

10 …I want to be strong in the Lord, and in the power of his might.

11 Today I will put on the whole armour of God, that I may be able to stand against the wiles of the devil.

12 For we wrestle not against flesh and blood, but against principalities, against powers, against the rulers of the darkness of this world, against spiritual wickedness in high [places].

13 Wherefore take I unto ME the whole armour of God, that I may be able to withstand in the evil day, and having done all, to stand.

14 I WILL stand therefore, having MY loins girt about with truth, and having on the breastplate of righteousness;

15 And MY feet shod with the preparation of the gospel of peace;

16 Above all, taking the shield of faith, wherewith I shall be able to quench all the fiery darts of the wicked.

17 And take the helmet of salvation, and the sword of the Spirit, which is the word of God:

18 Praying always with all prayer and supplication in the Spirit, and watching thereunto with all perseverance and supplication for all saints;

19 And for me, that utterance may be given unto me, that I may open my mouth boldly, to make known the mystery of the gospel,

20 For which I am an ambassador… that therein I may speak boldly, as I ought to speak.

CONCLUSION

Understanding the power of personal, daily prayer is a truly joyous and transformative journey. I want to emphasize that this book is merely a starting point, not an exhaustive compilation of prayers. Its purpose is to launch you into the depths of your own structured prayer life. I strongly encourage you to take the time to create your own prayer book or list, which you can bring with you into your prayer closet for intimate communion with God.

When someone requests your prayers, confidently assure them that you will intercede on their behalf. Write down their names and needs in your prayer book and faithfully lift them up before the Lord. This practice will deepen your connection with God, and enable His power to work through you.

I am thrilled by your passionate desire and eagerness for prayer. It is my sincere hope that every reader of this book will be filled with excitement and enthusiasm, not only to gain knowledge about prayer, but also to actively participate in it. Let us "pray without ceasing" as stated in 1 Thessalonians 5:17.

Whenever thoughts arise, let us turn them into prayers (as Bishop Joel Holmes refers to them as "gleaning prayers" in his book, *6 Steps to Prayer*). Let us also remember that it is equally important to acknowledge the significance of longer periods exclusively dedicated to concentrated prayer, without any distractions in your chosen place of solitude.

Prayer is our most powerful and potent tool, eagerly waiting for us to fully utilize it. I wholeheartedly believe in you as you embark on this journey through "The Whole Man." May the Lord abundantly bless you as He responds to your heartfelt prayers.

Made in the USA
Columbia, SC
20 January 2025

52154569R00059